ALZHEIMER UNFOLDING

Building Defenses Against Alzheimer's

NANCY JUDY

COPYRIGHT

TABLE OF CONTENTS

ABOUT THE BOOK

Alzheimer Unfolding is an extensive and compassionate exploration of Alzheimer's disease, offering a comprehensive guide to understanding, managing, and preventing this complex condition. Drawing on personal anecdotes, scientific insights, and practical advice, the book is a valuable resource for individuals, families, and caregivers navigating the challenges of Alzheimer's.

The book begins by introducing readers to Alzheimer's disease, unraveling its impact on individuals and families with empathetic storytelling and scientific detail. It provides an in-depth look at the disease's progression, symptoms, and the stages of cognitive decline, blending engaging language with expert knowledge to paint a vivid picture of the Alzheimer's journey.

Fueling Brain Health

One of the core sections of the book focuses on "Fueling Brain Health". It delves into the Alzheimer's prevention diet, emphasizing nutritional guidelines that support brain longevity. Readers learn about the importance of antioxidants, omega-3 fatty acids, and other brain-boosting nutrients, with practical dietary recommendations and meal plans designed to enhance cognitive vitality. The book also highlights superfoods and dietary supplements that can support cognitive function, offering recipes and meal planning tips to make brain-healthy eating accessible and enjoyable.

The section on "Physical Exercise for Brain Health" illustrates the profound benefits of physical activity on cognitive resilience. It includes tailored exercise routines and fitness programs for individuals with Alzheimer's, emphasizing how regular exercise can improve brain function and overall well-being.

The Vital Role of Caregivers and Family

In "The Vital Role of Caregivers and Family", the book acknowledges the crucial role caregivers and family members play in managing Alzheimer's. It explores the challenges and rewards of caregiving, offering strategies for self-care and support resources to help caregivers maintain their well-being. This section also addresses the importance of family involvement in Alzheimer's prevention, including goal-setting and lifestyle changes that promote brain health. Additionally, it covers legal and financial considerations, providing practical advice on estate planning, advance directives, and financial planning for families facing Alzheimer's.

Taking Control of Your Brain Health

"Taking Control of Your Brain Health" empowers readers to take proactive steps towards maintaining and enhancing cognitive function. This section outlines personalized brain health action plans, goal-setting strategies, and practical tips for integrating brain-healthy habits into daily routines. It covers various aspects of brain health, including nutrition, physical activity, mental stimulation, social engagement, stress management, and sleep. Through a blend of personal stories and scientific research, the book encourages readers to embrace a holistic approach to brain health.

Alzheimer Unfolding is more than just a guide—it's a beacon of hope and a source of knowledge for anyone impacted by Alzheimer's disease. With its empathetic approach, practical advice, and engaging narrative, the book provides readers with the tools they need to understand and manage Alzheimer's, support loved ones, and take control of their brain health for a better future.

INTRODUCTION

Alzheimer's disease is a profound and relentless journey, both for those who experience it and for those who care for them. As the most common form of dementia, Alzheimer's affects millions of people worldwide, transforming vibrant lives into a landscape of confusion, memory loss, and cognitive decline. Yet, within this challenging reality lies a world of hope, discovery, and the possibility of proactive intervention. "Alzheimer Unfolding" is a comprehensive exploration of this disease, designed to illuminate the multifaceted aspects of Alzheimer's while offering practical guidance for navigating its complexities.

In this book, we delve deeply into the intricacies of Alzheimer's disease, not only to understand its impact but also to empower readers with knowledge and strategies to take control of their brain health. From exploring the mechanisms behind the disease to outlining actionable steps for prevention and care, "Alzheimer Unfolding" serves as both a guide and a source of inspiration.

Alzheimer's disease is characterized by a progressive decline in cognitive function, marked by memory loss, confusion, and behavioral changes. Understanding the nature of this condition is crucial for both those affected and their caregivers. In the early chapters of "Alzheimer Unfolding", we explore the fundamentals of Alzheimer's disease, including its causes, risk factors, and the stages of progression. We examine the latest scientific insights into the disease's underlying mechanisms, such as the buildup of amyloid plaques and tau tangles in the brain, and the impact these changes have on cognitive function.

Empowering Through Knowledge

Knowledge is a powerful tool in the fight against Alzheimer's disease. Armed with information, individuals and families can make informed decisions about prevention, care, and treatment. "Alzheimer Unfolding" provides an in-depth look at various aspects of the disease, from genetic predispositions and lifestyle risk factors to current research and emerging treatments. By understanding these elements, readers are better equipped to take proactive steps toward maintaining cognitive health and managing the challenges associated with Alzheimer's.

Taking Control of Your Brain Health

One of the central themes of this book is the concept of proactive brain health. It is not only about managing Alzheimer's disease but also about taking deliberate actions to enhance brain function and reduce the risk of cognitive decline. "Alzheimer Unfolding" offers practical strategies for integrating brain-healthy habits into daily life, including nutrition, physical activity, mental stimulation, and social engagement. We provide personalized action plans and goal-setting strategies that empower readers to create a tailored approach to their brain health.

The Role of Caregivers and Family

Caregivers and family members are often the unsung heroes in the journey with Alzheimer's disease. Their role is both challenging and rewarding, requiring immense patience, compassion, and resilience. In "Alzheimer Unfolding", we address the unique challenges faced by caregivers and offer practical advice for self-care, support, and maintaining a balanced life. We explore the importance of building a supportive network, collaborating with healthcare providers, and planning for the future with legal and financial considerations.

Building a Supportive Network

A supportive network is essential for both individuals with Alzheimer's and their caregivers."*Alzheimer Unfolding" emphasizes the importance of family involvement in prevention strategies and the need for effective communication with healthcare providers. We offer guidance on creating a supportive environment, accessing community resources, and leveraging support networks to enhance care and well-being.

Navigating Legal and Financial Aspects

Planning for the future is a critical component of managing Alzheimer's disease. This book provides detailed information on estate planning, advance directives, and financial management. By addressing these legal and financial aspects, "Alzheimer Unfolding" helps readers protect their future and ensure that their wishes are honored.

An Invitation to Hope and Action

"Alzheimer Unfolding" is more than just a guide; it is an invitation to take action and embrace hope. Through personal anecdotes, scientific insights, and practical tips, we aim to immerse readers in the world of Alzheimer's with empathy and understanding. Our goal is to inspire proactive steps toward brain health, support caregivers, and foster a sense of community and resilience.

As you embark on this journey through "Alzheimer Unfolding", we invite you to explore, learn, and engage with the content. Whether you are seeking to understand Alzheimer's disease, looking for ways to enhance brain health, or navigating the complexities of caregiving, this book provides the tools and knowledge to empower you.

Together, we can unravel the complexities of Alzheimer's disease, embrace proactive approaches to brain health, and support one another in the face of this challenging condition. "Alzheimer Unfolding" is your guide to navigating this journey with hope, resilience, and a commitment to making a difference in your life and the lives of those you care about.

CHAPTER 1

UNVEILING ALZHEIMER'S DISEASE

Introduction to Alzheimer's Disease: A Journey Through the Mind

Imagine waking up one day and finding that the familiar faces and places that once brought you comfort and joy have become hazy and distant. This unsettling reality is what many individuals face when they embark on the journey through Alzheimer's disease. Named after Dr. Alois Alzheimer, who first described it in 1906, this neurodegenerative disorder is characterized by the progressive loss of cognitive function, particularly memory. It isn't merely a disease of forgetfulness; it's a profound alteration in the brain's ability to function, leading to significant changes in personality, behavior, and the ability to perform everyday tasks.

Alzheimer's disease affects millions of people worldwide, casting a long shadow not only over those diagnosed but also over their families and caregivers. It's a journey through the mind that demands resilience, love, and an unyielding hope for a cure.

Impact on Individuals and Families: Stories of Resilience and Love

When John noticed that his wife, Susan, began forgetting small things—misplacing her keys, repeating questions—he dismissed it as part of aging. But when she started getting lost on familiar routes and struggling with words, the reality of Alzheimer's disease became impossible to ignore. For John and Susan, as for countless other couples, Alzheimer's was a thief in the night, slowly stealing the essence of who Susan was.

Yet, within these stories of loss, there are also remarkable tales of resilience and love. Families often rally around their loved ones, creating a supportive network that helps navigate the turbulent waters of Alzheimer's. They find new ways to communicate, cherish moments of clarity, and adapt to the ever-changing landscape of the disease. Support groups, counseling, and educational resources become lifelines, providing solace and practical advice to those walking this difficult path.

One such story is of Maria, who moved in with her mother, Rosa, after her Alzheimer's diagnosis. Maria transformed her home into a sanctuary, filled with familiar objects and routines that provided Rosa with a sense of security. Together, they spent afternoons looking through old photo albums, allowing Rosa's memories to surface and providing moments of connection and joy.

Understanding Alzheimer's: Decoding the Enigma

Historical Context and Breakthroughs in Alzheimer's Research

The story of Alzheimer's disease begins in 1906 when Dr. Alois Alzheimer, a German psychiatrist and neuropathologist, presented the case of Auguste Deter, a woman who had experienced severe memory loss, confusion, and unpredictable behavior. Upon her death, Dr. Alzheimer examined her brain and discovered abnormal clumps (amyloid plaques) and tangled bundles of fibers (neurofibrillary tangles). These findings laid the foundation for understanding the pathological hallmarks of Alzheimer's disease.

Since then, research has made significant strides. The identification of genetic markers, such as the APOE ε4 allele, and the development of imaging techniques like PET scans, have revolutionized our understanding of the disease. Recent breakthroughs include the discovery of the role of tau proteins in forming neurofibrillary tangles and the impact of chronic inflammation on the brain.

Neurological Mechanisms Underlying Alzheimer's Progression

Alzheimer's disease is marked by the accumulation of amyloid-beta plaques and tau tangles in the brain. Amyloid-beta plaques form when fragments of a protein called amyloid precursor protein (APP) clump together outside neurons, disrupting cell function. Tau tangles occur inside neurons when tau proteins, which normally help stabilize microtubules, become abnormally phosphorylated and form twisted strands that disrupt the neuron's transport system.

These pathological changes lead to the death of neurons and the breakdown of synaptic connections, which are critical for memory and cognitive function. The brain's ability to communicate and process information deteriorates, leading to the symptoms observed in Alzheimer's patients.

Causes and Risk Factors: Unraveling the Mysteries Within

Genetic Predisposition and Environmental Influences

The exact cause of Alzheimer's disease remains elusive, but it is believed to result from a complex interplay of genetic, environmental, and lifestyle factors. Certain genetic mutations, particularly in the APP, PSEN1, and PSEN2 genes, are known to cause early-onset Alzheimer's, which appears before age 65. The APOE ε4 allele is the most significant genetic risk factor for late-onset Alzheimer's, increasing the likelihood of developing the disease.

Environmental factors also play a role. Chronic exposure to air pollution, head injuries, and cardiovascular conditions such as hypertension and diabetes have been linked to an increased risk of Alzheimer's. Additionally, lifestyle choices, such as diet, exercise, and cognitive engagement, significantly influence the likelihood of developing the disease.

Lifestyle Factors Contributing to Alzheimer's Risk

A growing body of research suggests that adopting a healthy lifestyle can reduce the risk of Alzheimer's. Regular physical activity, a balanced diet rich in fruits, vegetables, and omega-3 fatty acids, and maintaining social connections are all associated with a lower risk of cognitive decline. Engaging in mentally stimulating activities, such as reading, puzzles, and learning new skills, can also help preserve cognitive function.

Conversely, factors like smoking, excessive alcohol consumption, and a sedentary lifestyle can increase the risk of Alzheimer's. Managing chronic health conditions, such as hypertension and diabetes, is also crucial, as these conditions can exacerbate the risk of cognitive decline.

Symptoms and Stages: Navigating the Alzheimer's Landscape

Early Warning Signs and Subtle Changes

Alzheimer's disease often begins with subtle changes that can easily be mistaken for normal aging. Early symptoms include memory lapses, such as forgetting recently learned information, misplacing items, and struggling to find the right words. These changes can lead to confusion, disorientation, and difficulties in planning or solving problems.

As the disease progresses, individuals may experience changes in mood and behavior, becoming anxious, agitated, or depressed. They may also withdraw from social activities, lose interest in hobbies, and struggle with tasks that require concentration.

Progression Through Mild Cognitive Impairment to Advanced Stages

Alzheimer's disease progresses through several stages, each marked by increasing cognitive decline and functional impairment. The stages are often categorized as mild, moderate, and severe.

In the mild stage, individuals experience memory loss and cognitive difficulties that interfere with daily life. They may struggle with organizing tasks, making decisions, and remembering appointments.

In the moderate stage, symptoms become more pronounced. Individuals may have difficulty recognizing friends and family, become disoriented, and require assistance with daily activities such as dressing, eating, and bathing. Behavioral changes, such as aggression and wandering, are also common.

In the severe stage, individuals lose the ability to communicate, recognize loved ones, and perform basic functions. They become entirely dependent on caregivers for all aspects of daily living and may require round-the-clock care.

Cognitive Function and Daily Living: The Unseen Battles

Impact on Memory, Reasoning, and Decision-Making

Alzheimer's disease profoundly affects cognitive functions, with memory being the most significantly impacted. Short-term memory loss is often the first noticeable symptom, but as the disease progresses, long-term memory also deteriorates. Individuals may forget important dates, conversations, and even personal history.

Reasoning and decision-making abilities are also compromised. People with Alzheimer's may struggle to follow instructions, solve problems, and make sound judgments. This can lead to challenges in managing finances, driving, and navigating complex social situations.

Challenges in Performing Everyday Tasks and Maintaining Independence

Performing everyday tasks becomes increasingly difficult for individuals with Alzheimer's. Routine activities, such as cooking, cleaning, and shopping, become overwhelming. Even basic self-care tasks, like dressing and grooming, can pose significant challenges.

Maintaining independence is a constant struggle. As cognitive function declines, individuals may require assistance with tasks they once performed effortlessly. This loss of independence can be distressing and impact their sense of identity and self-worth.

Caregivers play a vital role in supporting individuals with Alzheimer's. They provide practical assistance, emotional support, and create a structured environment that minimizes confusion and anxiety. Simple adaptations, such as using labels, establishing routines, and creating a safe living space, can make a significant difference in the quality of life for both the individual with Alzheimer's and their caregiver.

Treatment Options and Limitations: Bridging the Gap to Hope

Pharmacological and Non-Pharmacological Interventions

Currently, there is no cure for Alzheimer's disease, but various treatments aim to alleviate symptoms and slow disease progression. Pharmacological treatments include cholinesterase inhibitors (such as donepezil, rivastigmine, and galantamine) and NMDA receptor antagonists (such as memantine). These medications can temporarily improve cognitive function and manage behavioral symptoms, but their effectiveness varies among individuals.

Non-pharmacological interventions are equally important in managing Alzheimer's. Cognitive stimulation therapy, which involves engaging in activities that stimulate thinking and memory, has shown positive effects on cognitive function. Behavioral interventions, such as creating a calm environment and using validation therapy, can help manage agitation and anxiety.

Emerging Therapies and Ongoing Research Efforts

The quest for more effective treatments and ultimately a cure for Alzheimer's is ongoing. Researchers are exploring various avenues, including targeting amyloid-beta plaques, tau tangles, and neuroinflammation. Immunotherapies, such as monoclonal antibodies, aim to clear amyloid plaques from the brain, showing promise in early clinical trials.

Additionally, advances in gene editing techniques, like CRISPR-Cas9, offer hope for addressing genetic risk factors associated with Alzheimer's. Lifestyle interventions, such as diet and exercise, continue to be studied for their potential to reduce risk and improve cognitive function.

Despite the challenges, there is optimism that ongoing research will lead to breakthroughs that transform the landscape of Alzheimer's treatment. Clinical trials, innovative therapies, and a growing understanding of the disease's mechanisms bring hope to millions affected by Alzheimer's.

Alzheimer's disease is a journey through the mind, marked by profound cognitive decline, emotional challenges, and the enduring strength of individuals and their families.

CHAPTER 2

THE POWER OF PREVENTION AND EARLY INTERVENTION

Promoting Brain-Healthy Habits and Lifestyle Modifications

Prevention is often the best defense against Alzheimer's disease, and a growing body of research suggests that adopting a brain-healthy lifestyle can significantly reduce the risk. While there is no guaranteed way to prevent Alzheimer's, making informed lifestyle choices can build a strong shield against this debilitating condition.

Diet and Nutrition

A brain-healthy diet is a cornerstone of Alzheimer's prevention. The Mediterranean diet, rich in fruits, vegetables, whole grains, fish, and healthy fats, has been associated with a reduced risk of cognitive decline. This diet emphasizes foods high in antioxidants and omega-3 fatty acids, which protect brain cells from damage and inflammation. Studies have shown that individuals who adhere to the Mediterranean diet have a lower incidence of Alzheimer's and other forms of dementia.

Physical Activity

Regular physical activity is another critical component of Alzheimer's prevention. Exercise increases blood flow to the brain, promotes the growth of new neurons, and enhances the brain's ability to repair itself. Aerobic exercises, such as walking, swimming, and cycling, have been shown to improve cognitive function and reduce the risk of cognitive decline. Even moderate activities like gardening and dancing can make a significant difference.

Mental Stimulation

Keeping the brain active and engaged is crucial for maintaining cognitive health. Activities that challenge the mind, such as puzzles, reading, and learning new skills, can help build cognitive reserves and delay the onset of Alzheimer's. Lifelong learning and continuous mental engagement stimulate neural connections and improve brain plasticity.

Importance of Cognitive Stimulation and Social Engagement

Cognitive Stimulation

Cognitive stimulation involves engaging in activities that challenge thinking and memory. Research has shown that individuals who regularly participate in mentally stimulating activities have a lower risk of developing Alzheimer's. Activities like playing musical instruments, learning new languages, and engaging in strategic games (e.g., chess, bridge) promote cognitive health.

Social Engagement

Social interaction is equally important for brain health. Maintaining strong social connections and participating in group activities can reduce the risk of Alzheimer's. Social engagement provides emotional support, reduces stress, and enhances cognitive function. People who are socially active are less likely to experience loneliness and depression, which are risk factors for cognitive decline.

For instance, Margaret, a retired teacher, joined a local book club and a gardening group after her husband's death. The social interactions and mentally stimulating activities provided her with a sense of purpose and helped her stay cognitively sharp. Studies support this, showing that socially engaged individuals have a lower risk of Alzheimer's.

Early Intervention: The Key to Unlocking Progress

Diagnostic Tools and Screening Methods for Early Detection

Early detection of Alzheimer's disease is crucial for implementing timely interventions that can slow disease progression and improve quality of life. Advances in diagnostic tools and screening methods have made it possible to identify Alzheimer's at its earliest stages.

Cognitive Assessments

Cognitive assessments, such as the Mini-Mental State Examination (MMSE) and the Montreal Cognitive Assessment (MoCA), are commonly used to evaluate memory, problem-solving, and other cognitive functions. These tests can help detect early signs of cognitive decline and determine the need for further evaluation.

Biomarkers

Biomarkers are biological indicators that can reveal the presence of Alzheimer's disease before symptoms become apparent. Amyloid-beta and tau proteins, which accumulate in the brains of individuals with Alzheimer's, can be measured in cerebrospinal fluid and blood. Advanced imaging techniques, such as PET scans and MRI, can detect amyloid plaques and brain atrophy, providing valuable information for early diagnosis.

Genetic Testing

Genetic testing can identify individuals at higher risk for Alzheimer's due to genetic mutations or the presence of the APOE ε4 allele. While genetic testing is not recommended for everyone, it can be useful for individuals with a family history of early-onset Alzheimer's.

Benefits of Timely Intervention in Slowing Disease Progression

Pharmacological Interventions

Early intervention with pharmacological treatments can help manage symptoms and slow disease progression. Cholinesterase inhibitors (such as donepezil, rivastigmine, and galantamine) and NMDA receptor antagonists (such as memantine) are commonly prescribed to improve cognitive function and manage behavioral symptoms. These medications are most effective when started in the early stages of Alzheimer's.

Non-Pharmacological Interventions

Non-pharmacological interventions play a crucial role in early intervention. Cognitive stimulation therapy, physical exercise, and lifestyle modifications can enhance cognitive function and delay the progression of Alzheimer's. Early intervention with these approaches can improve quality of life and help individuals maintain independence for longer.

For example, Robert, diagnosed with mild cognitive impairment (MCI), began a comprehensive intervention program that included cognitive training, a Mediterranean diet, and regular exercise. Over time, his cognitive decline slowed, and he was able to continue his daily activities with minimal assistance.

Stages of Alzheimer's: Mapping the Terrain of Change

Cognitive Decline and Behavioral Changes in Each Stage

Alzheimer's disease progresses through several stages, each characterized by increasing cognitive and functional decline. Understanding these stages can help caregivers and healthcare providers tailor interventions to manage symptoms and enhance quality of life.

Early Stage

In the early stage, individuals experience mild cognitive impairment and memory loss. They may forget recent events, struggle with words, and have difficulty with complex tasks. Despite these challenges, they can still perform most daily activities independently. Behavioral changes, such as mood swings and irritability, may also occur.

Middle Stage

The middle stage is marked by more pronounced cognitive decline and increased dependence on caregivers. Individuals may have difficulty recognizing family and friends, become disoriented, and require assistance with daily activities like dressing and bathing. Behavioral symptoms, such as agitation, aggression, and wandering, become more common.

Late Stage

In the late stage, individuals lose the ability to communicate, recognize loved ones, and perform basic functions. They become entirely dependent on caregivers for all aspects of daily living and may require round-the-clock care. Physical symptoms, such as difficulty swallowing and loss of mobility, also emerge.

Strategies for Managing Symptoms and Enhancing Quality of Life

Person-Centered Care

Person-centered care involves tailoring interventions to the individual's preferences, needs, and abilities. This approach enhances quality of life by focusing on the person's strengths and providing meaningful activities that promote engagement and well-being. For example, if an individual enjoys music, incorporating music therapy into their care plan can provide comfort and joy.

Environmental Modifications

Creating a supportive environment can help manage symptoms and reduce stress. Simple modifications, such as using labels and signs, minimizing clutter, and establishing a daily routine, can improve safety and reduce confusion. Ensuring that the living space is well-lit and free of hazards can prevent accidents and promote independence.

Behavioral Interventions

Behavioral interventions can help manage symptoms such as agitation, aggression, and anxiety. Techniques like validation therapy, where caregivers acknowledge the person's feelings and provide reassurance, can reduce distress. Activities that promote relaxation, such as gentle exercise, massage, and aromatherapy, can also help manage behavioral symptoms.

Coping with Diagnosis: Embracing the New Normal

Emotional Reactions and Psychological Adjustments to Diagnosis

Receiving an Alzheimer's diagnosis is a life-changing event that can evoke a range of emotional reactions, including shock, fear, anger, and sadness. It's essential for individuals and their families to acknowledge these feelings and seek support to navigate this challenging time.

Emotional Reactions

After her diagnosis, Linda felt a profound sense of loss and fear about the future. She worried about becoming a burden to her family and losing her independence. These emotional reactions are common and natural. It's important to allow oneself to grieve and process the diagnosis.

Psychological Adjustments

Adjusting to a diagnosis of Alzheimer's involves finding new ways to cope with the changes it brings. Accepting the diagnosis and focusing on what can be controlled can help individuals and their families find a sense of purpose and hope. Engaging in positive activities, maintaining social connections, and seeking professional guidance can support psychological adjustment.

Building a Support Network and Seeking Professional Guidance

Support Groups

Support groups provide a safe space for individuals with Alzheimer's and their caregivers to share experiences, express emotions, and receive practical advice. Connecting with others who are facing similar challenges can reduce feelings of isolation and provide valuable insights into managing the disease.

Professional Guidance

Healthcare professionals, such as neurologists, geriatricians, and social workers, can offer guidance on managing Alzheimer's and accessing resources. Counseling and therapy can help individuals and families cope with emotional challenges and develop effective coping strategies.

For instance, after joining a support group and receiving counseling, Linda felt more empowered to face her diagnosis. She gained practical tips for managing her symptoms and found comfort in knowing she was not alone.

Adjusting to Progression: Finding Strength in Every Step

Adaptive Strategies for Coping with Evolving Challenges

As Alzheimer's disease progresses, individuals and their caregivers must continually adapt to new challenges. Implementing adaptive strategies can help manage symptoms and maintain quality of life.

Daily Routines

Establishing a consistent daily routine can provide structure and reduce confusion. Regular schedules for meals, activities, and rest can help individuals with Alzheimer's feel more secure and oriented. Simple tasks, like laying out clothes in the order they should be worn, can promote independence

Assistive Devices

Assistive devices, such as pill organizers, reminder alarms, and mobility aids, can support individuals with Alzheimer's in managing daily activities. These tools can enhance safety and independence, allowing individuals to perform tasks with less assistance.

Resilience-Building Techniques and Maintaining a Sense of Purpose

Mindfulness and Relaxation Techniques

Practicing mindfulness and relaxation techniques can help individuals with Alzheimer's and their caregivers manage stress and improve well-being. Techniques like deep breathing, meditation, and yoga promote relaxation and emotional balance.

Engaging in Meaningful Activities

Engaging in meaningful activities that align with the individual's interests and abilities can enhance quality of life.

CHAPTER 3

SEEKING SOLUTIONS AND HOPE

Global Impact of Alzheimer's and the Need for Increased Awareness

Alzheimer's disease is a global crisis affecting millions of individuals and their families. According to the World Health Organization (WHO), over 50 million people worldwide are living with dementia, and Alzheimer's disease is the most common form. This number is expected to triple by 2050, highlighting the urgency for a solution.

The impact of Alzheimer's extends beyond individuals to families, communities, and healthcare systems. It is a leading cause of disability and dependency among older adults, placing a significant emotional, physical, and financial burden on caregivers. The cost of care for Alzheimer's patients is staggering, with global expenses projected to reach $1 trillion by 2030.

Increasing awareness about Alzheimer's is crucial for early detection, treatment, and support. Public health campaigns, educational programs, and media coverage play vital roles in spreading knowledge about the disease, reducing stigma, and encouraging people to seek help. Raising awareness can also drive policy changes and funding for research, ultimately bringing us closer to a cure.

Advocacy Efforts and Research Initiatives Driving Towards a Cure

Advocacy groups, such as the Alzheimer's Association and Alzheimer's Disease International, are at the forefront of efforts to combat Alzheimer's. These organizations work tirelessly to raise awareness, support patients and caregivers, and advocate for increased research funding.

Research initiatives have made significant strides in understanding Alzheimer's and developing potential treatments. The Alzheimer's Disease Neuroimaging Initiative (ADNI) has provided valuable insights into the disease's progression through advanced imaging techniques. The U.S. National Institutes of Health (NIH) and the European Union Joint Programme on Neurodegenerative Disease Research (JPND) have invested heavily in Alzheimer's research, leading to breakthroughs in genetics, biomarkers, and therapeutic strategies.

Despite these advancements, the search for a cure remains a race against time. Scientists are exploring various avenues, including immunotherapies, gene editing, and neuroprotective agents. Clinical trials are ongoing, testing new drugs and interventions that could slow or halt the disease's progression. The urgency for a solution drives researchers, healthcare professionals, and advocates to work collaboratively, pushing the boundaries of science and innovation.

Improving Cognition: Tools and Techniques for Brain Health

Cognitive Training Exercises and Memory Enhancement Strategies

Cognitive training exercises are designed to enhance memory, attention, problem-solving, and other cognitive functions. These exercises can help individuals maintain or improve their cognitive abilities, potentially delaying the onset of Alzheimer's or slowing its progression.

Brain Games and Puzzles

Engaging in brain games and puzzles, such as crosswords, Sudoku, and jigsaw puzzles, stimulates mental activity and strengthens neural connections. These activities challenge the brain, promoting cognitive resilience and flexibility

Memory Techniques

Memory enhancement strategies, such as mnemonic devices, visualization, and association, can improve recall and retention of information. Techniques like creating mental images, forming associations between concepts, and organizing information into meaningful patterns can enhance memory performance.

Cognitive Stimulation Therapy (CST)

Cognitive stimulation therapy involves structured group activities designed to stimulate thinking and social interaction. CST has been shown to improve cognitive function and quality of life for individuals with mild to moderate dementia. Activities include word games, discussions, and reminiscence therapy, which engage the mind and promote social connection.

Nutritional Supplements and Brain-Boosting Foods for Cognitive Function

Nutrition plays a crucial role in maintaining brain health and cognitive function. Certain foods and supplements have been shown to support brain health and may reduce the risk of cognitive decline.

Omega-3 Fatty Acids

Omega-3 fatty acids, found in fatty fish (such as salmon, mackerel, and sardines), flaxseeds, and walnuts, are essential for brain health. They reduce inflammation, support neuronal function, and promote the growth of new brain cells. Studies have linked higher omega-3 intake to a lower risk of Alzheimer's and improved cognitive function.

Antioxidant-Rich Foods

Antioxidant-rich foods, such as berries, leafy greens, and nuts, protect the brain from oxidative stress and inflammation. Antioxidants, including vitamins C and E, flavonoids, and polyphenols, neutralize free radicals and reduce the damage they cause to brain cells.

Nutritional Supplements

Certain supplements, such as curcumin (found in turmeric), resveratrol (found in red grapes), and phosphatidylserine, have shown promise in supporting cognitive function. Curcumin has anti-inflammatory and antioxidant properties, while resveratrol may enhance brain plasticity and protect against neurodegeneration. Phosphatidylserine, a phospholipid, supports cell membrane integrity and cognitive function.

Protecting Brain Health: Nurturing the Mind's Garden

Lifestyle Modifications for Brain Health and Cognitive Longevity

Adopting a brain-healthy lifestyle involves making informed choices that support cognitive function and reduce the risk of Alzheimer's.

Regular Physical Activity

Regular physical activity is one of the most effective ways to protect brain health. Exercise increases blood flow to the brain, promotes the growth of new neurons, and enhances cognitive function. Aerobic exercises, such as walking, running, and swimming, are particularly beneficial for brain health.

Healthy Diet

A healthy diet rich in fruits, vegetables, whole grains, lean proteins, and healthy fats supports brain health. The Mediterranean diet, in particular, has been associated with a lower risk of Alzheimer's. This diet emphasizes plant-based foods, healthy fats (such as olive oil), and lean proteins (such as fish and poultry).

Mental Stimulation

Engaging in mentally stimulating activities, such as reading, puzzles, and learning new skills, can help maintain cognitive function. Lifelong learning and continuous mental engagement stimulate neural connections and improve brain plasticity.

Stress Management Techniques and Mindfulness Practices for Brain Wellness

Chronic stress can negatively impact brain health and increase the risk of cognitive decline. Managing stress through mindfulness practices and relaxation techniques can support brain wellness.

Mindfulness Meditation

Mindfulness meditation involves focusing on the present moment and accepting it without judgment. This practice can reduce stress, improve emotional regulation, and enhance cognitive function. Regular mindfulness meditation has been shown to increase gray matter density in brain regions associated with learning, memory, and emotional regulation.

Relaxation Techniques

Relaxation techniques, such as deep breathing, progressive muscle relaxation, and guided imagery, can help manage stress and promote brain health. These techniques activate the body's relaxation response, reducing stress hormones and promoting a sense of calm.

Stress-Reducing Activities

Engaging in stress-reducing activities, such as yoga, tai chi, and spending time in nature, can support brain health. These activities promote relaxation, enhance mood, and improve overall well-being.

Communication Strategies: Connecting Beyond Words

Enhancing Communication Skills and Fostering Meaningful Interactions

Effective communication is essential for maintaining meaningful relationships and providing support for individuals with Alzheimer's. As the disease progresses, communication challenges become more pronounced, requiring caregivers to adopt strategies that enhance understanding and connection.

Active Listening

Active listening involves fully concentrating on the speaker, showing empathy, and providing feedback. This technique helps individuals with Alzheimer's feel heard and understood. Caregivers can use non-verbal cues, such as eye contact and nodding, to show engagement and support.

Simplifying Language

Simplifying language and using clear, concise sentences can help individuals with Alzheimer's understand and respond more effectively. Avoiding complex instructions and breaking tasks into smaller steps can also improve comprehension.

Non-Verbal Communication

Non-verbal communication, such as gestures, facial expressions, and touch, can convey emotions and support understanding. Smiling, holding hands, and using reassuring gestures can provide comfort and reinforce positive interactions.

Techniques for Effective Communication with Individuals in Different Stages of Alzheimer's

Early Stage

In the early stage of Alzheimer's, individuals may experience mild memory loss and difficulty finding words. Caregivers can support communication by providing cues, repeating information as needed, and encouraging the use of memory aids, such as notebooks and calendars.

Middle Stage

In the middle stage, communication challenges become more pronounced. Individuals may struggle with word retrieval, understanding complex instructions, and expressing themselves. Caregivers can use visual aids, such as pictures and gestures, to support communication. Patience and flexibility are essential, as individuals may need more time to process information and respond.

Late Stage

In the late stage, verbal communication becomes increasingly difficult. Caregivers can focus on non-verbal communication, using touch, facial expressions, and tone of voice to convey emotions and provide comfort. Music, sensory activities, and familiar objects can also facilitate connection and engagement.

For example, Emily found that her mother, Sarah, who was in the late stage of Alzheimer's, responded positively to music from her youth. Playing familiar songs and singing along helped Sarah feel more relaxed and connected. Even though verbal communication was limited, the shared experience of music provided a meaningful way to connect.

Seeking solutions and hope for Alzheimer's disease requires a multifaceted approach that includes prevention, early intervention, and ongoing support. By promoting brain-healthy habits, advancing research, and enhancing communication, we can improve the lives of those affected by Alzheimer's and work towards a future where this devastating disease is a thing of the past.

Through empathy, understanding, and a commitment to innovation, we can build a brighter future for individuals with Alzheimer's and their families.

CHAPTER 4

NAVIGATING EMOTIONS AND ENVIRONMENT

Understanding Emotional Fluctuations and Managing Challenging Behaviors

Alzheimer's disease is not just a journey through cognitive decline but also an emotional rollercoaster for both the individual and their loved ones. Mood swings and emotional distress are common, often exacerbated by the confusion and frustration that come with memory loss and cognitive impairment.

Understanding Emotional Fluctuations

Individuals with Alzheimer's experience a range of emotions, often cycling through happiness, anger, sadness, and fear within short periods. These emotional fluctuations can be triggered by various factors, including:

- Confusion and Disorientation: As cognitive abilities decline, the inability to make sense of their environment or recognize familiar faces can cause significant distress.
- Communication Barriers: Difficulty in expressing thoughts and needs can lead to frustration and feelings of isolation.
- Physical Discomfort: Pain, hunger, or other physical needs that are not easily communicated can manifest as agitation or aggression.

Environmental Changes: Moving to a new place or altering the home environment can provoke anxiety and confusion.

To illustrate, consider the case of John, a retired engineer diagnosed with Alzheimer's. His wife, Mary, noticed that John often became agitated in the late afternoon, a phenomenon known as "sundowning." Understanding that changes in light and routine might contribute to this behavior, Mary adjusted their daily schedule to include calming activities during these hours, which helped mitigate John's distress.

Managing Challenging Behaviors

Managing the emotional and behavioral challenges of Alzheimer's requires patience, empathy, and effective strategies:

- Validation Therapy: Rather than correcting false statements or memories, validate the individual's feelings and gently steer the conversation. For example, if someone insists they need to go to work despite being retired, acknowledge their concern ("You must have been very dedicated to your job") before redirecting the conversation.
- Routine and Structure: Establishing a predictable daily routine can provide a sense of security and reduce anxiety. Consistent meal times, activities, and rest periods help create a stable environment.
- Redirection: When an individual becomes upset, redirect their attention to a different, enjoyable activity. This could be a favorite hobby, music, or a walk outside.
- Calm Environment: Minimize noise, clutter, and other environmental stressors that might overwhelm the individual. Soft lighting and soothing music can create a calming atmosphere.

For instance, Jane, whose father, Tom, had Alzheimer's, found that playing his favorite classical music helped calm him during periods of agitation. The familiar tunes seemed to provide comfort and reduce his anxiety, highlighting the power of tailored interventions.

Coping Strategies for Caregivers and Family Members Supporting Individuals with Alzheimer's

Caring for someone with Alzheimer's can be physically and emotionally exhausting. Caregivers often experience a range of emotions, from sadness and frustration to guilt and burnout. Implementing effective coping strategies is crucial for maintaining their well-being and providing the best care possible.

Seeking Support

Support Groups: Joining a support group can provide a safe space to share experiences, gain insights, and receive emotional support from others facing similar challenges. These groups offer a sense of community and understanding that can be immensely comforting.

Professional Help: Counseling and therapy can help caregivers process their emotions, develop coping strategies, and navigate the complexities of caregiving. Professional guidance can provide personalized support and practical advice.

Self-Care

- Respite Care: Taking regular breaks is essential for preventing caregiver burnout. Respite care services, whether through professional caregivers or support from family and friends, allow caregivers to rest and recharge.

- Healthy Lifestyle: Maintaining a healthy lifestyle, including regular exercise, a balanced diet, and sufficient sleep, can improve caregivers' physical and emotional resilience. Exercise, in particular, is a powerful stress reliever and mood enhancer.

Education and Training

- Knowledge and Skills: Educating themselves about Alzheimer's disease, its progression, and effective caregiving techniques can empower caregivers to handle challenges more effectively. Many organizations offer training programs and resources for caregivers.

- Adaptability: Flexibility and adaptability are key to managing the unpredictable nature of Alzheimer's. Being open to changing strategies and trying new approaches can help caregivers respond to the evolving needs of their loved ones.

For example, Lisa, who cared for her mother with Alzheimer's, found solace in a local caregiver support group. Sharing her experiences and hearing from others provided emotional relief and practical tips that made her caregiving journey more manageable.

Room Design for Comfort: Creating Safe Havens for the Mind

Adaptive Home Modifications and Sensory-Friendly Environments

Creating a safe and comfortable environment is crucial for individuals with Alzheimer's. Thoughtful home modifications and sensory-friendly designs can enhance their quality of life and reduce stress and confusion.

Safety First

- Eliminate Hazards: Remove or secure items that pose a risk, such as sharp objects, loose rugs, and electrical cords. Ensure that walkways are clear and well-lit to prevent falls.
- Install Safety Features: Features like grab bars in the bathroom, non-slip mats, and locks on cabinets containing hazardous substances can enhance safety. Consider installing motion-sensor lights for better visibility at night.
- Emergency Preparedness: Ensure that emergency contacts and medical information are easily accessible. Equip the home with smoke detectors, carbon monoxide detectors, and fire extinguishers.

Promote Familiarity

- Personal Items: Surrounding individuals with familiar items, such as photographs, favorite books, and cherished mementos, can provide comfort and a sense of continuity.
- Consistent Layout: Maintaining a consistent furniture layout helps individuals navigate their environment more easily. Avoid frequent rearrangements that can cause confusion.

Sensory-Friendly Design

- Lighting: Use soft, natural lighting to create a calm and inviting atmosphere. Avoid harsh fluorescent lights that can be disorienting. Nightlights can help prevent confusion and accidents during nighttime.

- Colors: Choose soothing colors for walls and furnishings. Soft blues, greens, and pastels are calming, while avoiding overly bright or complex patterns can prevent overstimulation.

- Sound: Minimize background noise and create quiet spaces where individuals can retreat when feeling overwhelmed. Soft, soothing music can provide comfort and reduce agitation.

- For instance, Paul noticed that his wife, Anne, who has Alzheimer's, was calmer and more oriented in their living room filled with family photos and her favorite quilt. By maintaining a familiar environment and reducing sensory overload, Paul helped Anne feel more secure and at ease.

Creating Calming Spaces and Promoting Familiarity for Individuals with Alzheimer's

Designing specific areas of the home to promote relaxation and familiarity can significantly enhance the well-being of individuals with Alzheimer's.

Calming Spaces

- Relaxation Room: Designate a room or a corner as a relaxation space, equipped with comfortable seating, soft lighting, and calming décor. This space can be used for activities like reading, listening to music, or simply unwinding.

- Nature Elements: Incorporating elements of nature, such as plants, flowers, and views of the outdoors, can have a soothing effect. If possible, create an accessible garden or outdoor space where individuals can enjoy fresh air and nature.

Promoting Familiarity

- Personalized Touches: Incorporate personal items and familiar objects into the living space. Items like favorite books, family photos, and cherished mementos can evoke positive memories and provide comfort.
- Routine and Rituals: Establishing daily routines and rituals can create a sense of predictability and security. Consistent mealtimes, bedtime routines, and regular activities help individuals know what to expect and reduce anxiety.

For example, Emily created a "memory wall" in her father's room, filled with photos, postcards, and memorabilia from his past. This wall became a focal point for reminiscing and storytelling, providing comfort and sparking cherished memories.

Navigating the emotional and environmental challenges of Alzheimer's disease requires a compassionate and adaptive approach. Understanding and managing emotional fluctuations, creating safe and familiar environments, and implementing effective coping strategies can significantly enhance the quality of life for individuals with Alzheimer's and their caregivers. By fostering empathy, promoting comfort, and embracing flexibility, we can create supportive spaces that honor the dignity and individuality of those affected by this challenging disease. Through shared experiences, practical insights, and a commitment to compassionate care, we can make the journey through Alzheimer's more navigable and hopeful.

CHAPTER 5

FUELING BRAIN HEALTH

Nutritional Guidelines and Dietary Recommendations for Brain Health

Diet plays a crucial role in maintaining brain health and potentially reducing the risk of Alzheimer's disease. A well-balanced diet rich in specific nutrients can support cognitive function, reduce inflammation, and protect against neurodegenerative processes.

Mediterranean Diet

The Mediterranean diet is often cited as one of the best for brain health. It emphasizes fruits, vegetables, whole grains, nuts, seeds, lean proteins (especially fish), and healthy fats like olive oil. This diet is rich in antioxidants, anti-inflammatory compounds, and essential fatty acids.

DASH Diet

The Dietary Approaches to Stop Hypertension (DASH) diet, originally developed to lower blood pressure, has also shown benefits for brain health. It focuses on fruits, vegetables, whole grains, and lean proteins while limiting saturated fats, salt, and added sugars.

MIND Diet

The MIND (Mediterranean-DASH Intervention for Neurodegenerative Delay) diet combines elements of the Mediterranean and DASH diets specifically to boost brain health. It recommends high consumption of berries, leafy green vegetables, nuts, and olive oil, while limiting red meat, butter, cheese, pastries, and fried foods.

Key Nutritional Guidelines

- Fruits and Vegetables: Aim for a variety of colors to ensure a range of antioxidants and vitamins. Dark leafy greens and berries are particularly beneficial.
- Whole Grains: Choose whole grains over refined grains to provide fiber and essential nutrients.
- Lean Proteins: Incorporate fish, poultry, beans, and nuts as primary protein sources. Fish rich in omega-3 fatty acids, like salmon and mackerel, are especially beneficial.
- Healthy Fats: Use olive oil or other healthy fats instead of butter or margarine. Nuts, seeds, and avocados are also good sources of healthy fats.
- Limited Red Meat and Sweets: Reduce intake of red meat, processed foods, and sugary treats.

Importance of Antioxidants, Omega-3 Fatty Acids, and Brain-Boosting Nutrients

Antioxidants

Antioxidants help combat oxidative stress, a factor in the aging process and cognitive decline. Foods rich in antioxidants include:

- Berries: Blueberries, strawberries, and blackberries are high in flavonoids, which have been shown to improve memory.

- Leafy Greens: Spinach, kale, and broccoli contain vitamins E and C, which protect against oxidative damage.
- Nuts and Seeds: Almonds, walnuts, and sunflower seeds are packed with vitamin E, an important antioxidant for brain health.

Omega-3 Fatty Acids

Omega-3 fatty acids, particularly DHA (docosahexaenoic acid), are essential for brain health. They reduce inflammation, support neuronal function, and have been linked to a lower risk of Alzheimer's. Sources include:

- Fatty Fish: Salmon, mackerel, sardines, and trout.
- Flaxseeds and Chia Seeds: Plant-based sources of omega-3s.
- Walnuts: Another good plant-based source.

Brain-Boosting Nutrients

- Vitamin E: Found in nuts, seeds, and green leafy vegetables, it protects brain cells from oxidative damage.
- Vitamin B12: Important for maintaining healthy nerve cells, found in meat, fish, dairy, and fortified cereals.
- Folate: Found in leafy greens, legumes, and fortified grains, it supports cognitive function.

- Curcumin: The active ingredient in turmeric, curcumin has anti-inflammatory and antioxidant properties.

Brain-Boosting Nutrients: The Fuel for Cognitive Vitality

Superfoods and Dietary Supplements to Support Cognitive Function

Superfoods

- Blueberries: Rich in antioxidants, they improve memory and cognitive function.
- Spinach: High in vitamin K, folate, and antioxidants, it supports brain health.
- Walnuts: Provide omega-3 fatty acids, antioxidants, and polyphenols.
- Turmeric: Contains curcumin, which has anti-inflammatory and antioxidant properties.
- Green Tea: Contains L-theanine and polyphenols that improve brain function and protect against neurodegeneration.

Dietary Supplements

While a balanced diet is the best way to get essential nutrients, supplements can be beneficial when dietary intake is insufficient:

- Fish Oil: High in omega-3 fatty acids, supports brain health.
- Vitamin D: Important for brain function and often deficient in older adults.
- Ginkgo Biloba: May improve cognitive function and circulation.

- Phosphatidylserine: A phospholipid that supports cell membrane health and cognitive function.

Brain-Healthy Recipes

Breakfast: Berry and Nut Smoothie

Ingredients:

- 1 cup blueberries

- 1 banana

- 1 tablespoon almond butter

- 1 tablespoon chia seeds

- 1 cup spinach

- 1 cup almond milk

Instructions:

1. Blend all ingredients until smooth.

2. Serve immediately.

Lunch: Mediterranean Quinoa Salad

Ingredients:

- 1 cup cooked quinoa

- 1 cup cherry tomatoes, halved

- 1 cucumber, diced

- 1/4 cup red onion, finely chopped

- 1/4 cup Kalamata olives, pitted and sliced

- 1/4 cup feta cheese, crumbled

- 2 tablespoons olive oil

- Juice of 1 lemon

- Salt and pepper to taste

Instructions:

1. Combine quinoa, tomatoes, cucumber, red onion, olives, and feta in a bowl.

2. Drizzle with olive oil and lemon juice, then season with salt and pepper.

3. Toss to combine and serve.

Dinner: Baked Salmon with Spinach and Brown Rice

Ingredients:

- 2 salmon fillets

- 2 tablespoons olive oil

- 1 lemon, sliced

- 4 cups spinach

- 1 cup cooked brown rice

Instructions:

1. Preheat the oven to 375°F (190°C).

2. Place salmon on a baking sheet, drizzle with olive oil, and top with lemon slices.

3. Bake for 15-20 minutes, until salmon is cooked through.

4. Sauté spinach in a pan with a bit of olive oil until wilted.

5. Serve salmon with spinach and brown rice.

Meal Plan Example

Day 1

- Breakfast: Berry and Nut Smoothie

- Lunch: Mediterranean Quinoa Salad

- Dinner: Baked Salmon with Spinach and Brown Rice

- Snack: Handful of walnuts

Day 2

- Breakfast: Oatmeal with berries and almond butter

- Lunch: Mixed green salad with grilled chicken, avocado, and olive oil dressing

- Dinner: Lentil soup with whole grain bread

- Snack: Carrot sticks with hummus

Physical Exercise for Brain Health: Energizing the Mind and Body

Benefits of Physical Activity on Brain Function and Cognitive Resilience

Physical exercise is not only crucial for overall health but also plays a significant role in maintaining and enhancing brain function. Regular physical activity can:

- Improve Blood Flow: Exercise increases blood flow to the brain, delivering oxygen and nutrients that support cognitive function.

- Stimulate Neurogenesis: Physical activity promotes the growth of new neurons in the hippocampus, a brain region critical for memory and learning.

- Enhance Neuroplasticity: Exercise supports the brain's ability to adapt and reorganize itself, crucial for learning and memory.

- Reduce Inflammation: Physical activity helps lower levels of inflammation in the brain, which is linked to cognitive decline.

- Reduce Stress: Exercise releases endorphins, which can reduce stress and improve mood, positively affecting cognitive health.

Tailored Exercise Routines and Fitness Programs for Individuals with Alzheimer's

Aerobic Exercises

Aerobic exercises increase heart rate and improve cardiovascular health, which benefits brain function:

- Walking: A simple, accessible exercise that can be done daily. Aim for at least 30 minutes of brisk walking.
- Swimming: A low-impact exercise that is gentle on the joints and provides cardiovascular benefits.
- Cycling: Whether on a stationary bike or outdoors, cycling is excellent for cardiovascular health.

Strength Training

Strength training helps maintain muscle mass and supports overall physical health:

- Bodyweight Exercises: Squats, lunges, and push-ups can be done at home without any equipment.
- Resistance Bands: Using resistance bands can provide a safe and effective strength workout.

- Light Weights: Lifting light weights can improve muscle strength and coordination.

Flexibility and Balance

Flexibility and balance exercises can reduce the risk of falls and improve overall mobility:

- Yoga: Enhances flexibility, balance, and relaxation. Many yoga poses can be modified for different ability levels.
- Tai Chi: A gentle form of martial arts that focuses on slow, controlled movements and balance.
- Stretching: Incorporating regular stretching into a daily routine can improve flexibility and reduce muscle stiffness.

Exercise Program Example

Day 1: Aerobic Focus

- Warm-up: 5 minutes of light stretching
- Exercise: 30 minutes of brisk walking
- Cool-down: 5 minutes of gentle stretching

Day 2: Strength Training

- Warm-up: 5 minutes of light stretching

- Exercise:

- - 3 sets of 10 squats

- - 3 sets of 10 lunges (each leg)

- - 3 sets of 10 push-ups (modified if

CHAPTER 6

THE VITAL ROLE OF CAREGIVERS AND FAMILY

Challenges and Rewards of Caregiving for Individuals with Alzheimer's

Caregiving for individuals with Alzheimer's disease is a journey fraught with challenges, yet also rich with profound rewards. This journey demands immense patience, compassion, and resilience, often requiring caregivers to balance the emotional and physical tolls of providing care.

Challenges of Caregiving

- Emotional Strain: Watching a loved one's cognitive decline can be heart-wrenching. Caregivers often experience grief, sadness, and frustration as they cope with the progressive loss of the person they once knew.

- Physical Demands: The physical tasks of caregiving—helping with mobility, personal hygiene, and daily activities—can be exhausting, especially as the disease advances.

- Financial Burden: Alzheimer's care can be expensive. The costs of medical treatment, specialized care, and potential loss of income due to caregiving responsibilities can create significant financial strain.

- Isolation: Caregivers may feel isolated, as their responsibilities can limit their ability to maintain social connections and participate in activities they once enjoyed.

- Burnout: The relentless demands of caregiving can lead to burnout, characterized by physical exhaustion, emotional fatigue, and decreased ability to provide quality care.

Rewards of Caregiving

Despite these challenges, many caregivers find profound rewards in their role:

- Deepened Bonds: Caregiving can strengthen the emotional bond between the caregiver and the person with Alzheimer's, fostering moments of connection and love.
- Sense of Purpose: Providing care can instill a sense of purpose and fulfillment, knowing that they are making a meaningful difference in their loved one's life.
- Personal Growth: Caregivers often develop resilience, patience, and empathy, gaining valuable insights and perspectives through their experiences.
- Legacy of Love: Many caregivers take pride in honoring their loved one's legacy, ensuring they are treated with dignity and respect.

For instance, Sarah, who cared for her mother with Alzheimer's, shared how the experience brought her family closer together. Despite the emotional and physical challenges, she found solace in the moments of joy and connection they shared, cherishing her mother's smile and the simple pleasures of spending time together.

Self-Care Strategies and Support Resources for Caregivers

Taking care of oneself is crucial for caregivers to sustain their ability to provide care. Implementing self-care strategies and seeking support can help caregivers manage stress and prevent burnout.

Self-Care Strategies

- Regular Breaks: Schedule regular breaks to rest and recharge. Short periods of respite can make a significant difference in maintaining energy and focus.

- Healthy Lifestyle: Prioritize a balanced diet, regular exercise, and adequate sleep. These habits improve physical health and emotional resilience.

- Mindfulness and Relaxation: Practice mindfulness, meditation, or yoga to manage stress and promote relaxation. Even a few minutes of deep breathing can help reduce anxiety.

- Hobbies and Interests: Engage in activities and hobbies that bring joy and fulfillment. Maintaining personal interests can provide a sense of normalcy and escape.

- Social Connections: Stay connected with friends and family. Regular social interactions can provide emotional support and reduce feelings of isolation.

Support Resources

- Support Groups: Join support groups for caregivers, either in-person or online. These groups offer a sense of community, shared experiences, and practical advice.

- Respite Care: Utilize respite care services to take a break from caregiving duties. Temporary relief can be provided by professional caregivers, adult day care centers, or family and friends.

- Professional Counseling: Seek counseling or therapy to address emotional challenges and develop coping strategies. Professional guidance can offer personalized support.

- Educational Resources: Access educational resources and training programs to learn about Alzheimer's disease, caregiving techniques, and available support services.

For example, John found immense support in a local caregiver group where he met others facing similar challenges. Sharing stories, exchanging tips, and receiving encouragement helped him navigate the complexities of caregiving and reminded him that he was not alone in his journey.

Family Involvement in Alzheimer's Prevention and Risk Reduction Strategies

Family members play a vital role in Alzheimer's prevention and risk reduction. By fostering a supportive environment and adopting healthy lifestyle practices, families can collectively work towards reducing the risk of Alzheimer's.

Promoting Healthy Lifestyles

- Balanced Diet: Encourage a diet rich in fruits, vegetables, whole grains, lean proteins, and healthy fats. The Mediterranean and DASH diets are excellent models for brain-healthy eating.
- Physical Activity: Promote regular physical exercise, such as walking, swimming, or cycling. Exercise supports cardiovascular health and cognitive function.
- Cognitive Stimulation: Engage in activities that challenge the brain, such as puzzles, reading, and learning new skills. Cognitive stimulation helps maintain mental sharpness.
- Social Engagement: Foster social connections and participation in community activities. Social engagement has been linked to better cognitive health.
- Stress Management: Practice stress-reducing techniques, such as mindfulness, meditation, and relaxation exercises. Chronic stress can negatively impact brain health.

Education and Awareness

- Stay Informed: Educate family members about Alzheimer's disease, its risk factors, and prevention strategies. Knowledge empowers individuals to make informed choices.

- Regular Health Check-Ups: Encourage regular health check-ups and screenings. Early detection of risk factors, such as hypertension and diabetes, can lead to timely interventions.

- Genetic Counseling: For families with a history of Alzheimer's, consider genetic counseling to understand genetic risks and potential preventive measures.

For example, the Garcia family made a collective effort to adopt a healthier lifestyle after learning about their genetic predisposition to Alzheimer's. They began cooking more nutritious meals together, participating in family exercise routines, and engaging in mentally stimulating activities like board games and puzzles.

Communication and Collaboration with Healthcare Providers and Support Networks

Effective communication and collaboration with healthcare providers and support networks are essential for managing Alzheimer's and implementing prevention strategies.

Building a Healthcare Team

- Primary Care Physician: Maintain regular appointments with a primary care physician who can monitor overall health and manage risk factors.

- Neurologist: Consult a neurologist for specialized care related to cognitive health and Alzheimer's disease.

- Dietitian/Nutritionist: Seek advice from a dietitian or nutritionist to develop a brain-healthy diet plan.

- Mental Health Professional: Engage with a mental health professional for counseling and support with emotional challenges.

Effective Communication

- Be Honest and Open: Share concerns, symptoms, and family history with healthcare providers. Honest communication ensures comprehensive care.

- Ask Questions: Don't hesitate to ask questions and seek clarification about diagnoses, treatments, and prevention strategies.

- Document Information: Keep a record of medical appointments, test results, medications, and care plans. Organized documentation helps in managing care and communicating with the healthcare team.

Collaboration with Support Networks

- Family Meetings: Hold regular family meetings to discuss caregiving responsibilities, health updates, and prevention strategies. Open communication fosters collaboration and shared decision-making.

- Community Resources: Utilize community resources, such as Alzheimer's associations, support groups, and respite care services. These resources provide valuable support and information.

- Online Forums: Participate in online forums and social media groups dedicated to Alzheimer's caregivers. These platforms offer a space to share experiences, seek advice, and connect with others.

For instance, the Johnson family worked closely with their healthcare team and support networks after their father's diagnosis. Regular family meetings ensured everyone was informed and involved in caregiving decisions, while community resources provided additional support and respite care options.

Estate Planning and Advance Directives for Individuals with Alzheimer's

Planning for the future is crucial when facing an Alzheimer's diagnosis. Legal and financial considerations should be addressed early to ensure the individual's wishes are honored and to provide financial security.

Estate Planning

- Will: Ensure that the individual has a valid will outlining the distribution of assets. A will can prevent legal disputes and ensure that assets are allocated according to the individual's wishes.

- Trusts: Establish trusts to manage and protect assets. Trusts can provide financial security and avoid probate.

- Power of Attorney: Designate a power of attorney (POA) for financial and healthcare decisions. A financial POA manages financial affairs, while a healthcare POA makes medical decisions if the individual becomes incapacitated.

- Living Will: Create a living will to specify medical treatment preferences in case of incapacity. This document guides healthcare providers and loved ones in making medical decisions.

Advance Directives

- Healthcare Proxy: Designate a healthcare proxy to make medical decisions on behalf of the individual if they are unable to do so.
- Do Not Resuscitate (DNR) Order: Consider a DNR order if the individual wishes to decline life-saving measures such as CPR.
- End-of-Life Care: Discuss preferences for end-of-life care, including hospice and palliative care options.

For example, Margaret's family ensured that she had a comprehensive estate plan and advance directives in place after her Alzheimer's diagnosis. These legal documents provided clarity and peace of mind, ensuring that her wishes were honored and her assets were protected.

Financial Planning and Long-Term Care Options for Families Facing Alzheimer's

Managing the financial aspects of Alzheimer's care requires careful planning to ensure the individual's needs are met without imposing an undue burden on the family.

Financial Planning

- Budgeting: Create a budget that includes all anticipated expenses, such as medical treatments, medications, home modifications, and caregiving services.

- Insurance: Review existing insurance policies, including health, life,

CHAPTER 7

TAKING CONTROL OF YOUR BRAIN HEALTH

Alzheimer's disease and other forms of dementia pose significant challenges to individuals and their families, but proactive steps toward brain health can empower individuals to take control of their future. By developing personalized action plans, setting realistic goals, and integrating brain-healthy habits into daily routines, people can enhance their cognitive resilience and potentially reduce the risk of Alzheimer's.

Personalized Brain Health Action Plans and Goal-Setting Strategies

Understanding Personal Risk Factors

The first step in taking control of brain health is understanding personal risk factors. These can include genetic predisposition, family history, lifestyle choices, and other health conditions. By recognizing these factors, individuals can tailor their brain health action plans to address specific areas of concern.

Creating a Brain Health Action Plan

A brain health action plan is a personalized strategy that outlines specific steps to maintain and improve cognitive function. Here are some key components of an effective plan:

1. Assessment and Baseline: Start with a comprehensive assessment of current cognitive function and overall health. This can be done through cognitive testing, medical evaluations, and

self-assessments. Establishing a baseline helps track progress and identify areas needing attention.

2. Goal Setting: Set specific, measurable, attainable, relevant, and time-bound (SMART) goals. These goals should address various aspects of brain health, such as nutrition, physical activity, mental stimulation, and social engagement. For example, a goal might be to walk 30 minutes a day, five days a week, or to learn a new hobby within three months.

3. Action Steps: Break down each goal into actionable steps. This makes goals more manageable and increases the likelihood of success. For instance, if the goal is to improve diet, action steps could include planning weekly meals, grocery shopping for brain-healthy foods, and preparing meals in advance.

4. Monitoring and Adjusting: Regularly review progress toward goals and adjust the action plan as needed. This could involve tracking dietary intake, exercise routines, and cognitive activities. Monitoring progress helps maintain motivation and allows for timely adjustments to the plan.

5. Support Systems: Engage family, friends, and healthcare providers in the brain health journey. Support systems provide encouragement, accountability, and assistance in achieving goals.

Goal-Setting Strategies

Effective goal setting involves understanding the principles of behavior change and motivation. Here are some strategies to enhance goal-setting success:

- Start Small: Begin with small, achievable goals that build confidence and momentum. Gradually increase the difficulty of goals as confidence and abilities grow.

- Be Specific: Clearly define what you want to achieve and how you will do it. Specific goals provide a clear direction and reduce ambiguity.

- Track Progress: Use journals, apps, or other tools to monitor progress. Tracking progress provides a sense of accomplishment and helps identify patterns and areas for improvement.

- Celebrate Success: Recognize and celebrate achievements, no matter how small. Celebrating success boosts motivation and reinforces positive behavior.

- Stay Flexible: Be prepared to adjust goals and action steps as needed. Flexibility allows for adapting to changing circumstances and maintaining progress.

Personal Anecdote

Maria, a 55-year-old woman with a family history of Alzheimer's, decided to take control of her brain health by creating a personalized action plan. She started by assessing her current lifestyle and identifying areas for improvement. Maria set specific goals, such as incorporating more vegetables into her diet, walking daily, and joining a book club for mental stimulation. By breaking these goals into actionable steps and tracking her progress, Maria felt empowered and motivated. Over time, she noticed improvements in her energy levels, mood, and cognitive function. Maria's proactive approach and commitment to her brain health inspired her family to join her in adopting healthier habits, creating a supportive environment for everyone.

Integrating Brain-Healthy Habits into Daily Routines and Lifestyle Choices

Nutrition

A brain-healthy diet is crucial for cognitive function and overall brain health. The Mediterranean and DASH diets are particularly beneficial, emphasizing whole foods, healthy fats, lean proteins, and plenty of fruits and vegetables.

- Fruits and Vegetables: Aim to fill half your plate with fruits and vegetables. These foods are rich in antioxidants, vitamins, and minerals that protect brain cells and reduce inflammation. Berries, leafy greens, and cruciferous vegetables are especially beneficial.
- Healthy Fats: Incorporate sources of healthy fats, such as olive oil, avocados, nuts, and seeds. Omega-3 fatty acids, found in fatty fish like salmon and flaxseeds, are essential for brain health.
- Whole Grains: Choose whole grains like brown rice, quinoa, and whole wheat bread over refined grains. Whole grains provide fiber and essential nutrients that support brain health.
- Lean Proteins: Include lean proteins such as fish, poultry, beans, and legumes in your diet. Protein is necessary for neurotransmitter function and overall brain health.
- Hydration: Stay hydrated by drinking plenty of water throughout the day. Dehydration can impair cognitive function and concentration.

Physical Activity

Regular physical activity is vital for maintaining cognitive function and overall health. Exercise increases blood flow to the brain, supports neurogenesis (the growth of new neurons), and reduces the risk of chronic diseases that can affect brain health.

- Aerobic Exercise: Engage in aerobic exercises like walking, jogging, swimming, or cycling for at least 150 minutes per week. These activities improve cardiovascular health and brain function.
- Strength Training: Incorporate strength training exercises, such as lifting weights or using resistance bands, at least twice a week. Strength training helps maintain muscle mass and supports overall physical health.
- Flexibility and Balance: Practice flexibility and balance exercises, such as yoga or tai chi, to improve coordination and reduce the risk of falls.

Mental Stimulation

Keeping the brain active and challenged is essential for cognitive health. Engaging in mentally stimulating activities can enhance neuroplasticity, the brain's ability to adapt and reorganize itself.

- Learning New Skills: Take up new hobbies or learn new skills, such as playing a musical instrument, painting, or speaking a new language. Learning new things stimulates different parts of the brain and keeps it engaged.

- Puzzles and Games: Solve puzzles, play chess, or engage in other strategic games that require critical thinking and problem-solving.

- Reading and Writing: Read books, articles, or write in a journal. These activities stimulate the brain and enhance cognitive function.

- Creative Activities: Engage in creative activities like drawing, crafting, or dancing. Creativity stimulates the brain and provides an outlet for expression.

Social Engagement

Social interaction is a critical component of brain health. Maintaining strong social connections and engaging in social activities can reduce the risk of cognitive decline and improve mental well-being.

- Stay Connected: Make an effort to stay connected with family and friends. Regular social interactions provide emotional support and mental stimulation.

- Join Groups: Participate in community groups, clubs, or organizations that interest you. These groups provide opportunities for socialization and shared activities.

- Volunteer: Volunteering for causes you care about can provide a sense of purpose and connect you with like-minded individuals.

- Family Activities: Engage in activities with family members, such as game nights, outings, or shared hobbies. Family activities strengthen bonds and create positive memories.

Stress Management

Chronic stress can negatively impact brain health, so it's essential to develop effective stress management techniques.

- Mindfulness and Meditation: Practice mindfulness or meditation to reduce stress and promote relaxation. Even a few minutes a day can make a significant difference.
- Relaxation Techniques: Engage in relaxation techniques such as deep breathing, progressive muscle relaxation, or guided imagery.
- Time Management: Improve time management skills to reduce stress and improve productivity. Prioritize tasks, set realistic deadlines, and take breaks when needed.
- Hobbies and Interests: Spend time on hobbies and activities you enjoy. Doing things you love can provide a sense of fulfillment and reduce stress.

Sleep

Adequate sleep is essential for cognitive function and overall health. Poor sleep can impair memory, concentration, and mood.

- Establish a Routine: Set a regular sleep schedule by going to bed and waking up at the same time each day.
- Create a Sleep-Friendly Environment: Ensure your bedroom is conducive to sleep by keeping it cool, dark, and quiet.
- Limit Stimulants: Avoid caffeine, nicotine, and other stimulants close to bedtime.

- Relax Before Bed: Develop a relaxing bedtime routine, such as reading, taking a warm bath, or practicing relaxation techniques.

Personal Anecdote

David, a 60-year-old man concerned about his brain health, decided to take proactive steps to maintain cognitive function. He began by integrating brain-healthy habits into his daily routine. David started his mornings with a nutritious breakfast rich in fruits, whole grains, and lean proteins. He incorporated regular exercise into his schedule, alternating between brisk walks and yoga sessions. David also joined a local book club and started learning to play the guitar, both of which provided mental stimulation and social interaction. To manage stress, David practiced mindfulness meditation for 10 minutes each evening. By making these changes, David felt more energized, focused, and confident in his ability to maintain his brain health as he aged.

Taking control of your brain health involves proactive steps, personalized action plans, and the integration of brain-healthy habits into daily routines. By understanding personal risk factors, setting specific goals, and engaging in activities that promote cognitive function, individuals can enhance their cognitive resilience and potentially reduce the risk of Alzheimer's disease. Whether through nutrition, physical activity, mental stimulation, social engagement, stress management, or sleep, each component plays a vital role in maintaining brain health. Embracing these habits empowers individuals

CONCLUSION

"Alzheimer Unfolding" delves deeply into the multifaceted world of Alzheimer's disease, unraveling its complexities with a blend of scientific insight, practical advice, and empathetic understanding. Through its comprehensive exploration of Alzheimer's, the book serves not only as an informative guide but also as a source of inspiration and hope.

- Understanding Alzheimer's Disease: The book begins by offering an extensive overview of Alzheimer's disease, including its impact on cognitive function and daily living. It explores the causes, risk factors, and progression of the disease, providing a thorough understanding of its biological and psychological dimensions. This foundation is crucial for readers to grasp the full scope of Alzheimer's and its effects on individuals and families.

- Fueling Brain Health: The book highlights the importance of nutrition, physical exercise, and mental stimulation in maintaining brain health. It provides actionable strategies for adopting a brain-healthy diet, engaging in regular physical activity, and incorporating cognitive exercises into daily routines. The emphasis on integrating these habits into a lifestyle underscores the role of proactive measures in potentially reducing the risk of Alzheimer's.

- The Role of Caregivers and Family: One of the most poignant sections of the book focuses on the unsung heroes of Alzheimer's care—caregivers and family members. It addresses the challenges and rewards of caregiving, offering practical tips for self-care and highlighting the importance of building a supportive network. The book also provides valuable insights into legal and financial considerations, helping families navigate the complexities of estate planning and long-term care.

- Taking Control of Your Brain Health: The final sections empower readers to take charge of their brain health through personalized action plans and goal-setting strategies. It encourages readers to make informed choices about nutrition, exercise, mental stimulation, and stress management, emphasizing that proactive steps can significantly impact cognitive vitality and overall well-being.

In Summary "Alzheimer Unfolding" is a comprehensive resource that combines scientific rigor with compassionate guidance. It empowers readers with knowledge and practical tools to understand, prevent, and manage Alzheimer's disease. By addressing every aspect of brain health—from diet and exercise to caregiving and legal considerations—the book offers a holistic approach to navigating the challenges of Alzheimer's and fostering a future of hope and resilience. Through its blend of personal anecdotes, expert insights, and actionable advice, "Alzheimer Unfolding" stands as a beacon of knowledge and support for those affected by Alzheimer's disease and their loved ones.